Who Lives in a Deep, Dark Cave?

Rachel Lynette

PowerKiDS press

New York

To Scott, who took me to see Carlsbad Caverns a very long time ago

Published in 2011 by The Rosen Publishing Group, Inc.
29 East 21st Street, New York, NY 10010

First Edition

Editor: Joanne Randolph
Book Design: Greg Tucker
Photo Researcher: Jessica Gerweck

Photo Credits: Cover Purestock/Getty Images; pp. 4, 6, 7, 9, 13, 14, 16, 18 Shutterstock.com; p. 5 Eastcott Momatiuk/Getty Images; p. 8 William Palmer/Getty Images; pp. 10–11 Ken Lucas/Getty Images; p. 12 Stephen Alvarez/Getty Images; p. 15 © Superstock/age fotostock; p. 17 John Lund/Getty Images; p. 19 Altrendo Travel/Getty Images; pp. 20–21 Joe Cornish/Getty Images; p. 22 John & Lisa Merrill/Getty Images.

Library of Congress Cataloging-in-Publication Data

Lynette, Rachel.
  Who lives in a deep, dark cave? / Rachel Lynette.
      p. cm. — (Exploring habitats)
  Includes index.
  ISBN 978-1-4488-0676-8 (library binding) — ISBN 978-1-4488-1277-6 (pbk.) —
ISBN 978-1-4488-1278-3 (6-pack)
  1. Cave animals—Juvenile literature. 2. Caves—Juvenile literature. I. Title.
  QL117.L96 2011
  591.75'84—dc22
                                                  2009052017

Manufactured in the United States of America

CPSIA Compliance Information: Batch #WS10PK: For Further Information contact Rosen Publishing, New York, New York at 1-800-237-9932

Contents

Into the Dark

What is it like in a cave? When you walk into a cave, you are entering a secret world of underground rooms and tunnels. It is very dark in a cave because the Sun's rays cannot reach very far inside.

Caves can have lakes in them. They can also have interesting rock shapes.

It is also cool inside a cave. Many caves can be wet as well. You may hear the sound of dripping water there.
Some caves are very big. They may have rooms the size of several football

fields or thousands of miles (km) of tunnels. Some caves are very small. Not every hollow space in the earth is a cave, though. Even a small cave must be large enough for a person to fit inside.

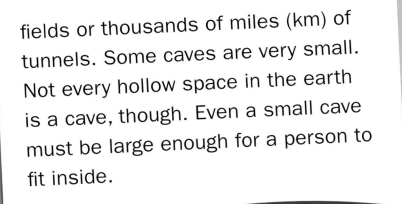

Caves can be formed from ice. This one in Antarctica was shaped by waves.

Life in a Cave

You would likely not want to live in a cave, but for some animals it is an excellent home. These animals have **adapted** to living in a dark, cold, and wet **habitat**.

Wolves, such as this one, often make their homes in caves.

Many animals live near the cave opening, where there is still some light and warmth from the Sun. Others live deep in the cave, where there is no light at all. Some cave animals live under rocks on the cave floor or hide in cracks, or small openings, in the cave walls. Some, like bats, hang from the ceiling. Other cave animals live in streams that run through caves. There are a lot more animals living in deep, dark caves than you may have thought!

This wallaby peeks out from its cave. The cave keeps animals such as wallabies safe from danger.

A Sunless Life

Some animals spend their whole lives deep in a cave. They are born inside the cave and never leave it. These animals are called troglobites.

Animals that spend their whole lives in caves never see the Sun.

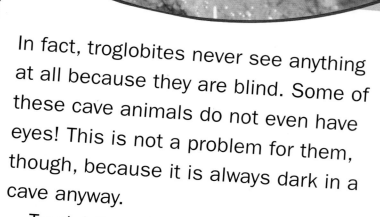

The Ozark blind salamander shown here is a troglobite. It likes caves with streams or water.

In fact, troglobites never see anything at all because they are blind. Some of these cave animals do not even have eyes! This is not a problem for them, though, because it is always dark in a cave anyway.

Troglobites have thin skin, and their skin is generally white or pink. This is because they do not need **protection** from the Sun. The smallest troglobites are insects, spiders, **crustaceans**, and flatworms. They become food for bigger troglobites, such as cave fish and blind salamanders.

This cave in Tennessee is likely home to the Tennessee cave salamander, which is the state's official amphibian.

Fish with No Eyes

Blind cave fish live in underground streams. They are only about 4 inches (10 cm) long. Blind cave fish do not have any eyes. Even though they are blind, cave fish can feel small **vibrations** in the water.

Can you find the eyes on this fish? You cannot find its eyes, because this blind cave fish, like others of its kind, does not have any!

These vibrations tell them where objects are. This helps keep them from swimming into things and helps them find food.

There is not a lot of food in a cave stream. This means that cave fish cannot be too picky. Blind cave fish will eat almost anything they can find. They will eat bits of leaves that wash into the stream from above ground. They also eat small animals like flatworms, insects, and blind crayfish. Blind cave fish will even eat their own babies!

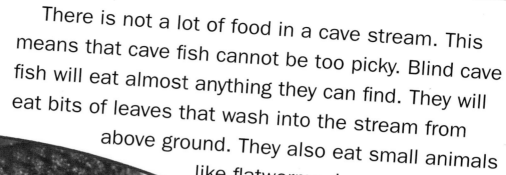

Cave Lovers

Some cave animals are called troglophiles, or cave lovers. These animals like dark, wet places and may spend their whole lives in caves. These animals are not troglobites, though, because they can also live outside the cave.

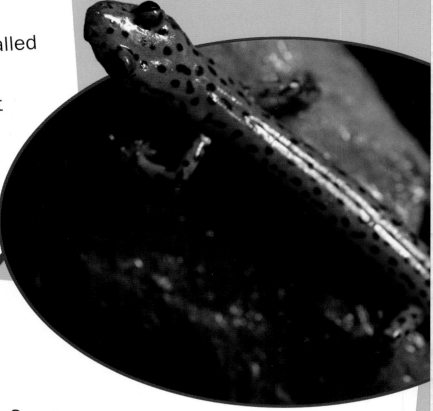

This cave salamander is a troglophile. Compare its eyes and bright colors to the salamander on page 8.

Small cave lovers include beetles, crickets, millipedes, spiders, daddy longlegs, and snails. Some frogs and salamanders are also cave lovers. Cave-loving animals often live near the opening of the cave where there is

some light. Some troglophiles that live in caves never leave the cave, while others go out at night to find food. Cave lovers that do not live in caves live under rocks or in other dark, wet places.

This frog lives in a cave. It may leave the cave sometimes, though, to look for food or a mate. A mate is another frog with which it can make babies.

Wingless Cave Crickets

Cave crickets are cave lovers. They do not have wings, as other crickets do. Instead, they have longer back legs than do most crickets. This lets them jump high and far. Cave crickets also

This cricket lives above the ground. You can see its wings folded on its back.

have extra long **antennae**. They move their antennae from side to side in front of them so they will not bump into anything in the darkness of the cave. Cave crickets eat whatever they can find inside or outside the caves where they live. Usually they eat bits of dead plants or animals. However, if a cave cricket cannot find enough to eat, it may eat one of its own legs! That is one hungry cricket!

This cave cricket has no wings and it has smaller eyes than its Sun-loving relative on page 14.

15

Just Visiting

Some animals use caves for shelter but do not spend their whole lives there. These animals are called trogloxenes. Most of these visiting animals do not go deep into the cave. They like to stay near the cave opening where they can still see.

Have you ever seen raccoons going through your trash at night? They do not spend all their time in caves, but they may use caves for shelter.

Some animals in this group, such as porcupines, raccoons, skunks, and foxes, generally live just outside a cave's opening. They may come into a cave to hide or for protection from the weather.

Pack rats build their nests inside caves. They build their nests from small sticks, stones, and other things that they find near the cave. Bears use caves to sleep during the cold winter months.

This bear is leaving the cave where it spent the winter. Bears find a cave where they can rest safely until warm weather comes again.

17

Just Hanging Out

Bats are important trogloxenes in the cave habitat. During the day, bats hang from the ceilings in the dark parts of caves. The bats' droppings, or **guano**, fall to the cave floor. Cave animals then eat the bat guano.

Bats, such as this one, spend their days hanging from cave ceilings or other dark places.

They also eat old and weak bats that fall off the cave ceiling. Without the bats, many troglobites would die of hunger.

Bats are important outside of the cave as well. At night the bats leave the cave and hunt for insects to eat.

At Carlsbad Caverns, in New Mexico, nearly a million Mexican free-tail bats leave the cave each evening during summer. A Mexican free-tail bat can eat half its weight in insects every night!

Carlsbad Caverns, shown here, is known for the large number of bats that live inside its rooms. There are 17 different kinds of bats in these caves.

What Grows in a Cave?

Green plants need sunlight to grow. Many plants grow just outside a cave. Ferns, mosses, and some kinds of **algae** can grow inside a cave, near its opening. Rain washes parts of these plants into

Here you can see the many different kinds of plants and mosses that can grow in a cave's opening.

the deeper parts of the cave. There they become food for hungry cave animals.

No green plants grow deep in a cave where there is no sunlight. **Fungi** and **bacteria** can grow in the dark parts of a cave, though. They do not need sunlight to grow. They get their energy from dead plants and animals or other matter. Caves that are wet can make an excellent home for fungi and bacteria.

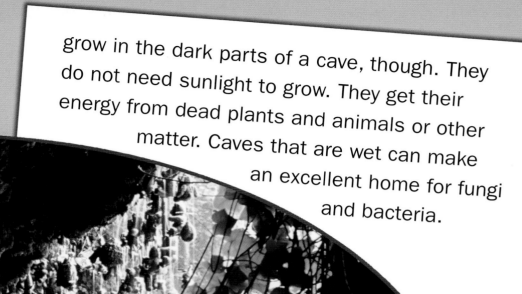

Exploring a Cave

Would you like to visit a cave? It can be fun to explore a cave. There are often beautiful rocks and interesting animals there. However, exploring a cave can be unsafe. Be sure to go with an adult and to use safety **equipment**.

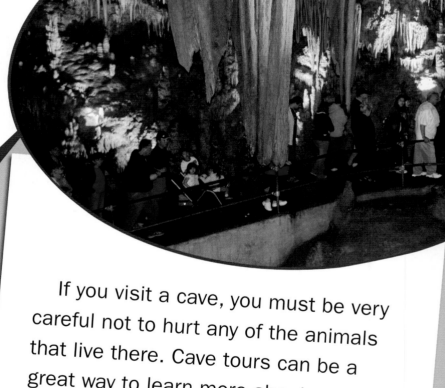

These people are taking a tour of a cave. Many caves have walkways and lighted parts so visitors can move through the cave safely.

If you visit a cave, you must be very careful not to hurt any of the animals that live there. Cave tours can be a great way to learn more about caves. Better still, cave tours keep people and animals safe!

Glossary

adapted (uh-DAPT-ed) Changed over time to help stay alive.

algae (AL-jee) Plantlike living things without roots or stems that live in water.

antennae (an-TEH-nee) Thin, rodlike feelers on the heads of certain animals.

bacteria (bak-TIR-ee-uh) Tiny living things that cannot be seen with the eye alone.

crustaceans (krus-TAY-shunz) Animals that have no backbones, have hard shells and other body parts, and live mostly in water.

equipment (uh-KWIP-mint) All the supplies needed to do something.

fungi (FUN-jy) Plantlike living things that do not have leaves, flowers, or green color and that do not make their own food.

guano (GWAH-noh) Bat droppings.

habitat (HA-beh-tat) The kind of land where an animal or a plant naturally lives.

protection (pruh-TEK-shun) Something that keeps something else from being hurt.

vibrations (vy-BRAY-shunz) Fast movements up and down or back and forth.

Index

A
algae, 20
animals, 6–8, 11–12,
    15–16, 18, 20–22
antennae, 14

B
bacteria, 20–21

C
cracks, 6
crustaceans, 9

E
equipment, 22

F
floor, 6, 18

fungi, 20–21

G
guano, 18

H
home, 6, 21

L
light, 6, 13

O
opening(s), 6, 12,
    16, 20

P
person, 5
protection, 9, 16

R
rocks, 6, 13, 22
rooms, 4

S
Sun, 4, 6, 8–9

T
troglobites, 8–9, 12,
    18
tunnels, 4–5

V
vibrations, 10

W
warmth, 6
water, 4, 10

Web Sites

Due to the changing nature of Internet links, PowerKids Press has developed an online list of Web sites related to the subject of this book. This site is updated regularly. Please use this link to access the list:
www.powerkidslinks.com/explore/ddc/